The Life and Work of ...

Paul Klee

Sean Connolly

Heinemann
LIBRARY

www.heinemann.co.uk/library

Visit our website to find out more information about Heinemann Library books.

To order:

 Phone 44 (0) 1865 888066

 Send a fax to 44 (0) 1865 314091

 Visit the Heinemann Bookshop at www.heinemann.co.uk/library to browse our catalogue and order online.

First published in Great Britain by Heinemann Library, Halley Court, Jordan Hill, Oxford OX2 8EJ, a division of Reed Educational and Professional Publishing Ltd. Heinemann is a registered trademark of Reed Educational and Professional Publishing Ltd.

OXFORD MELBOURNE AUCKLAND JOHANNESBURG BLANTYRE
GABORONE IBADAN PORTSMOUTH (NH) USA CHICAGO

Designed by Celia Floyd
Originated by Dot Gradations Ltd
Printed and bound by South China Printing in Hong Kong/China

ISBN 0 431 13162 7 (hardback)
06 05 04 03 02
10 9 8 7 6 5 4 3 2 1

ISBN 0 431 13167 8 (paperback)
06 05 04 03 02
10 9 8 7 6 5 4 3 2 1

British Library Cataloguing in Publication Data

Connolly, Sean
Life and work of Paul Klee
1. Klee, Paul, 1879–1940 – Juvenile literature
2. Painters – Switzerland – Biography – Juvenile literature
3. Painting, Modern – 20th Century – Switzerland – Juvenile literature
4. Painting, Swiss – Juvenile literature
I. Title
759.9'494

Acknowledgements

The publishers would like to thank the following for permission to reproduce photographs: AKG Photo, pp. 4, 10, 22, 24; Paul-Klee-Stiftung, Kunstmuseum, Bern/L Moillet, p.20. Fotopress/Walter Henggeler, p. 28; Page 5, Paul Klee *Familienspaziergang, 1930 26*, Credit: Paul-Klee-Stiftung, Kunstmuseum, Bern. Page 7, Paul Klee *Dünen Landschaft, 1923, 139*, Credit: Paul-Klee-Stiftung, Kunstmuseum, Bern. Page 9, Paul Klee *Schadau, 1893/96*, Credit: Paul-Klee-Stiftung, Kunstmuseum, Bern. Page 11, Paul Klee *Siebzehn, irr. 1923*, Credit: Oeffentliche Kunstsammlung Kupferstichkabinett, Basel. Page 13, Paul Klee *Meine Bude, 1896*, Credit: Paul-Klee-Stiftung, Kunstmuseum, Bern. Page 15, Paul Klee *Lily, 1905, 32*, Credit: Paul-Klee-Stiftung, Kunstmuseum, Bern. Page 17, Paul Klee, *Candide 7. Capitel "Il lève le voile d'une main timide" 1911, 63*', Credit: Paul-Klee-Stiftung, Kunstmuseum, Bern. Page 19, Paul Klee *Mädchen mit Krügen, 1910, 120*', Credit: Paul-Klee-Stiftung, Kunstmuseum, Bern. Page 21, Paul Klee *Rote und Weisse Kuppeln, 1914, 45*', Credit: AKG Photo. Page 23, Paul Klee *Einst dem Grau der Nacht enttaucht…, 1918, 17*', Credit: Paul-Klee-Stiftung, Kunstmuseum, Bern. Page 25, Paul Klee *Plan einer garten-architektur, 1920, 214*', Credit: Bridgeman Art Library. Page 27, Paul Klee *Polyphon gefasstes Weiss, 1930, 140(x10)*', Credit: Paul-Klee-Stiftung, Kunstmuseum, Bern. Page 29, Paul Klee *TOD und FEUER, 1940, 332 (G 12)*, Credit: Paul-Klee-Stiftung, Kunstmuseum, Bern.

Cover photograph: *Hauser am Meer*, 1920, reproduced with permission of AKG London.

Our thanks to Paul Flux, Sue Graves and Hilda Reed for their advice and expertise in the preparation of this book.

Every effort has been made to contact copyright holders of any material reproduced in this book. Any omissions will be rectified in subsequent printings if notice is given to the publishers.

Contents

Any words appearing in the text in bold, **like this**, are explained in the Glossary.

Who was Paul Klee?

Paul Klee was a Swiss painter and **graphic artist**. He liked to make very colourful paintings. His pictures make people think of music and dreams.

This is a photograph of Paul Klee.

Paul Klee

paintbrushes

Paul kept a sense of fun in his paintings. This picture shows how he liked to 'take a line for a walk'.

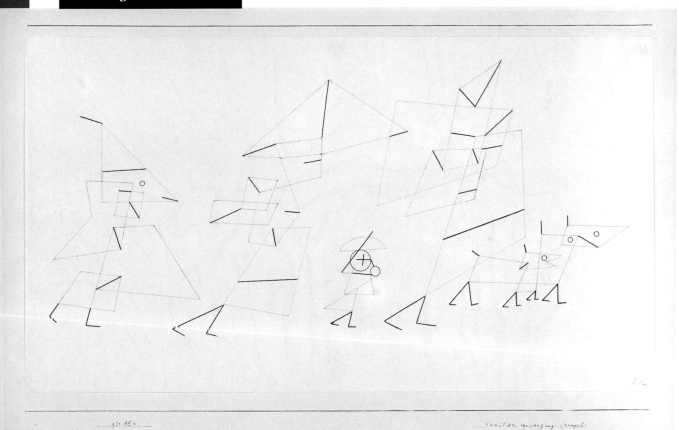

Klee produced this picture in 1930. Take a good look at it and you will see how the lines seem to be walking across the page.

Early years

Paul Klee was born on 18 December 1879 near the city of Berne in Switzerland. His family loved music.

Paul's parents were both musicians. Paul himself became a very good violinist.

Paul's mother

Paul

violin

Paul learned to play the violin when he was seven years old.

Paul's uncle Ernst had a café. As a young boy, Paul loved to look at the patterns on the tablecloths there.

Even as an adult, Klee was still interested in patterns. Work out how old he was when he painted this picture.

Dune Landscape, 1923

7

School-days

Paul went to school in Berne. He still enjoyed music and loved playing his violin.

Paul playing in the Berne **orchestra**.

Paul

violin

music

8

Paul also began to like drawing pictures. He filled his school notebooks with drawings and designs. He tried to show his love of music and poetry in his paintings.

Paul drew this picture in 1895 when he was only sixteen years old.

Paul drew this picture in a notebook.

The move to Germany

Paul left school when he was 19. He moved to Munich, Germany. There he began to **study** drawing and painting.

magazine

Magazines like this helped Klee to think of funny ideas.

Klee studied art in Munich from 1898 to 1901.

10

Klee had a good sense of humour. This picture was made in 1923 when he was 44 years old.

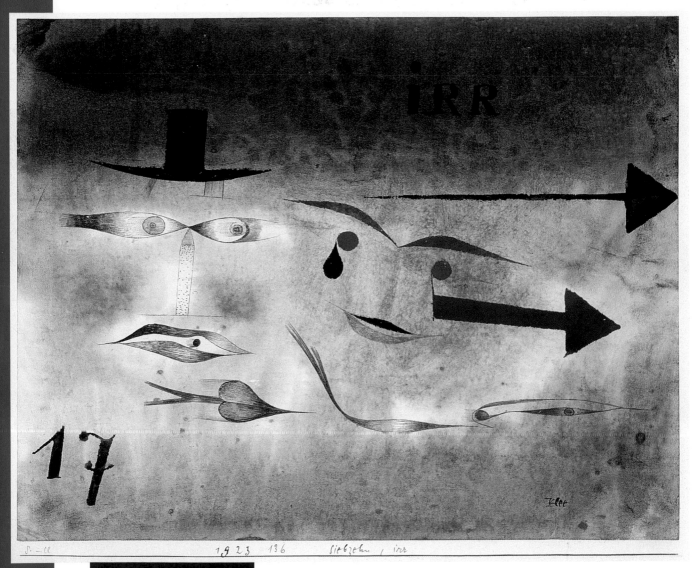

Seventeen, 1923

Learning to paint

Klee **studied** paintings in Italy when he was 22 years old. He then returned to his family in Berne. There he **practised** his own art and tried out many different ideas.

Klee studying Italian paintings.

Klee

Most of Klee's works were drawings or **etchings**. He could draw very well.

This picture of Klee's bedroom shows how well he could draw.

Meine Bude, 1896

A growing family

In 1906 Klee married Lily Stumpf. Their son Felix was born a year later. Lily earned money by playing piano **concerts**.

Klee worked at home after his marriage.

easel   canvas   Klee   Felix

Some of Klee's **etchings** were **exhibited** in Munich in 1906. Klee became better known after the exhibition.

This is a painting of Paul's wife, Lily.

Public success

Klee's first one-man **exhibition** was in Berne in 1910. It was a great success.

People enjoyed visiting Klee's exhibition.

Klee's paintings

Klee's one-man exhibition was also shown in other Swiss cities.

Klee's pictures were black and white. He used an ink pen and drew on white paper.

Notice how tall and thin Klee has drawn these figures.

This picture was used in a book.

A friendly welcome

Klee became friends with two other artists, August Macke and Wassily Kandinsky. In 1911 Klee joined their group of **expressionist** artists, called Der Blaue Reiter (The Blue Rider).

artists

Klee

Paul joined Der Blaue Reiter group.

Klee liked the work of other artists. This painting of his looks like a painting by the artist Paul Cezanne.

Woman with Jug, 1910

Cezanne's influence can be seen in this painting.

Colour takes hold

Paul Klee and August Macke in Tunisia.

In 1914 Klee and August Macke visited Tunisia in Africa. Klee loved the bright light and colours there. He decided to stop using just black and white in his pictures.

Red and White Domes, 1914

The coloured squares in this painting look like the mosaics Klee saw in Tunisia.

This painting shows how Klee began to use colours.
Work out how long ago that was.

New directions

Klee was happy painting in many colours. He felt free to try other new ideas too. He started putting letters and numbers in his pictures.

A photo of Klee in his studio with the paints he used.

Klee

paints

Klee thought numbers and letters made people think of words and dreams. He felt he was making a new **language** in his pictures.

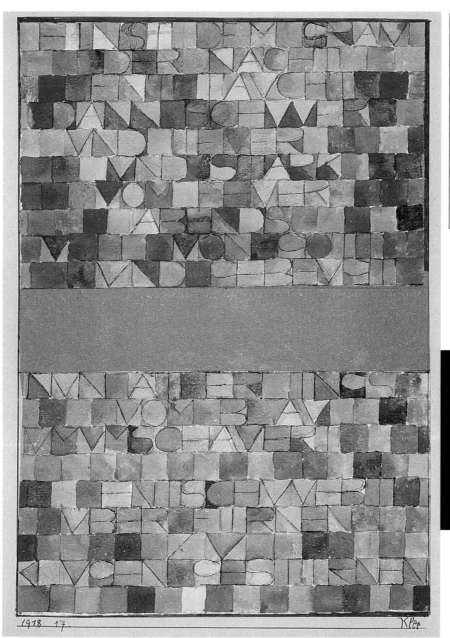

How many different letters and shapes can you see in this painting?

Once Emerged from the Grey of Night, 1918

23

Time as a teacher

Bauhaus
art school

The Bauhaus was the most famous art school in Germany.

In 1920 Klee became a teacher at the Bauhaus at Weimar and at Dessau. Klee taught there until 1931.

Plan of a Garden Design, 1920

Klee's pictures show what he taught at the Bauhaus. He taught students that an artist is like a tree trunk. The branches are the thoughts he shows in his pictures.

Escape from Germany

A new **government**, called the **Nazis**, took power in Germany. Their leader was Adolf Hitler. They did not like Klee's pictures. Klee had to move to Switzerland in 1933.

Nazi

Klee

The Nazis did not like Klee's pictures.

The Nazis wanted pictures to look like real things. Klee did not agree. He used his colours and lines to make people think for themselves.

27

Illness and death

Klee became ill when he was 56 years old. He never got better. He still painted but he was in constant pain.

Klee when he was very ill.

Klee died aged 61 on 29 June 1940.

28

Death and Fire, 1940

Klee's illness made him think about death and war. Thick black lines replaced the bright colours he had used when he was well.

Klee thought about death and war not only because he was ill but also because **World War II** was being fought at the time.

Timeline

1879	Paul Klee born near Berne, Switzerland on 18 December.
1886	Paul begins to **study** the violin.
1889	Klee joins Berne Municipal **Orchestra**.
1893	Lumière brothers develop cinema in France.
1898	Klee leaves school and moves to Munich, Germany.
	The sculptor Henry Moore is born.
1903	The Wright brothers fly the first aeroplane.
1906	Klee marries Lily Stumpf and has **etchings exhibited**.
	The artist Paul Cézanne dies.
1910	Klee has successful exhibitions in Switzerland.
1911	Klee joins The Blue Rider group of **expressionist** artists.
1913	Charlie Chaplin makes his first film.
1914	Klee visits Tunisia and starts to fill his pictures with colour.
1914–18	World War I.
1920–31	Klee teaches at the famous Bauhaus art school in Germany.
1926	The artists Claude Monet and Mary Cassatt die.
1927	Charles Lindbergh makes first solo flight across the Atlantic.
1933	Klee forced to leave Germany and go to Switzerland.
1935	Klee's long illness starts.
1939	**World War II** begins in Europe.
1940	Klee dies in Muralto, Switzerland on 29 June.

Glossary

concert playing music in public

etching picture made by drawing on a metal plate and then printing it

exhibit show and sell works of art in public

expressionist a type of art that changes the way things look to show feelings

government group of people who rule a country

graphic artist someone who makes pictures to print

language way of passing on ideas to other people

mosaics pattern of coloured stone used to make a picture

Nazi short name for the National Socialist German Workers' Party

World War II war involving many important nations, fought in Europe, Africa and Asia from 1939 to 1945

orchestra group of musicians who play concerts in public

practise keep trying to do something to get better at it

study learn about a subject

More books to read

How Artists Use Perspective, Paul Flux, Heinemann Library

The Life and Work of Wassily Kandinsky, Paul Flux, Heinemann Library

More paintings by Paul Klee to see

Comedy, Tate Modern, London

Seaside Resort in the South of France, Tate Modern, London

31

Index